Love, Pain and Other Clichés

AF624597

Chinzupe Phiri

BookLeaf Publishing

Love, Pain and Other Clichés © 2022

Chinzupe Phiri

All rights reserved.

No part of this publication may be reproduced, stored in a retrieval system, or transmitted, in any form or by any means, electronic, mechanical, photocopying, recording or otherwise, without the prior written permission of the presenters.

Chinzupe Phiri asserts the moral right to be identified as author of this work.

Presentation by *BookLeaf Publishing*

Web: www.bookleafpub.com

E-mail: info@bookleafpub.com

ISBN: 9789357445498

First edition 2022

DEDICATION

To everyone who told me to keep writing.

ACKNOWLEDGEMENT

A poet is nothing without a muse. Grateful for everyone who got me to laugh, made me cry, drove me to anger, sunk me to depression and stirred me to passion.

PREFACE

An honest exploration of both the internal and external challenges of entering adulthood. This compilation of poems have been written during some of the most turbulent times in my life. They are snapshots, streams of consciousness, confessions, theories and therapy sessions.

Tap dancing in the Tempest

Life right now is a tempest.
I want to rest but the temptress is draped in
fabrics that accentuate a shape resembling a
question mark, I'm kept busy by the quest.
At best I am a philosopher pondering how to
address these torturing cons to contend with,
The duress has me reaching for a durex but
feeling the full effect of a vice
is the only way you realise the price of
momentary pleasure is a cost that
doesn't feel nice to pay.

I'm tired of the games they play,
I'm tired because I never asked for things to be
this way,
I'm tired because although I'm dismayed,
staying this way will not help,
May dis become the light instead of the lagoon
that brings a darkness like the night with no
moon.
My eyes never monsoon and maybe that makes
my heart dry and brittle,

If I watered it maybe there'd be less of a
struggle, less tension, and I could grow or heal,
All the time I feel way too much -
drowning in sorrow he would hop, skip and
jump on,

So I seek him, wholly.
I must be him, holy.

Hard to do when I'm falling apart
and with the pieces I pick I don't know where to
start.
I take things to the heart and you take things
lightly,
You should give what you get and respond
politely,
I hope you can do things with me, not in spite of
me.

Muscle Memory

I remember I remember,
The touch that gave you tremors,
That spot to strike for a stellar review.
You took what I gave but that's not all I had for
you,
We both had walls we couldn't see through,
Until we were skin to skin it was hard to read
you,
The grip revealed more than our lips or what we
typed with fingertips,
Tripping over worries about falling too fast,
Scarred by bruises we had got in the past,
Young and only looking for fun but you became
the one
I'd stay with from moon 'til sun.

So it gets complicated, past what we anticipated,
All we did couldn't just be undone,
Out of our depths - we could take each other's
breath
but couldn't quite take each other's hand,
Hand's we'd both bitten, fingers we'd both
sucked,
But it was already written in the acts that
couldn't keep our thoughts tucked,

It was always easier behind closed doors.
Taking time giving every inch of mine and tasting what was yours,
For some reason we always found an excuse to bail,
so maybe we were always doomed to fail.
I wish you well as you go onto sail in the sea of existence,
I'll keep my distance,
Knowing now that separation is the best assistance I can give since I have still not learned to keep consistency,

Be well and be free.

Paper Thin

I'm worried I'm see through like paper when
tears drop and bleed through,
I grew up thinking telling someone "I need you,"
would be the quickest way to make them leave
you.
I've never been violent but always been volatile,
Craving touch,
I became tactile to communicate emotions I
couldn't say,
If I keep you within in arms reach you've slyly
got your way because I rarely make room for
people to stay,
I preferred to come and go on my own accord
and on travels abroad
I could be found beside a broad you hadn't seen
me with before,
Clever ones could see *that was* the curtain.
The smoke screen trick,
Continue being seen with a chick and you'll
never be still enough for them to see you're
hurting,
A paper thin veil was enough to create the ruse
and hide each bruise,
I was on cruise control until my body had to
snooze,

The cost of sleepless nights.
Losing hours to thoughts that chewed and consumed every sinew that was trying to deduce how I could keep the façade ice cold whilst my heart bubbled and fumed,
Ready to exude sentiments repressed to keep pretending things were cool.

Sometimes I feel split in two
Part of me grew in the light,
Darkness is the only thing the other part of me ever knew,
Both halves of me combined will be defined by these words I scribble between lines that tell my story in half rhymes,
One day I will return to worship the Lord's shrine and everything I've scribed will be left behind.
I hope whoever finds these papers can read it fine, then roll it up,
Burn it then return it to the ether as vapour,
Giving back to the universe,
What it gave me,
What I held as mine,

A Waltz in the Witching Hour

It’s not usually said so hastily.
There isn’t a rush to make it happen.
It doesn’t have to be now,
The voice speaks patiently, consistently
Using a reassuring tone that it’s the right thing to do,
Not just for me, for everybody,
Things might just be easier that way.
I’m allowed to bring my reasons, my arguments
I’m allowed to discuss and dissect because he knows that’s where he really gets me,
The inspection, when we analyse and pick it all apart.

The darkness stains and the light is fleeting,
Heat never infiltrates like the cold,
I can save myself from the piercing chill but at best
that leaves me numb.
It leaves me passive, impartial, nonchalant.
I feel sparks every now and then but it’s hard to get the circulation going

and keep it going.
Is there a point of having a chandelier when you can't keep the lights on?
The bells and whistles are pretty but they don't make me warm, nothing else can.

Nothing external,
but the voices -

They drag and drain, the lips that speak siphon life with every letter they shape and put together to sap my stores.

At this point I'm being kept in this play by the fact I don't want to make a scene.
We are always on stage, improvising,
Amending the script, or living up to it.
Everything is made up and perhaps the deeper we get into our own creations the realer this gets.
Artistic license should not be used sparingly.
Create, concoct, conjure, influence, imitate, endure.
You must contribute all the colours you can before you depart.
Duty.
You can abscond from your duty but we will see, we will know, you must choose,
Do you care?

Before Anything Else

Before anything else:
You are alone.
You may be the quilt of many independent
thoughts and ideas from a myriad of sources
Even still ultimately, intimately, you are one.

Some may mortgage your mind or find
residency in your heart,
Still solo.
So get comfortable at rock bottom,
Enjoy the sound of your thoughts hustling and
bustling to remind yourself of the shards of your
identity,
Hold up the glass to the light that shows your
true colour,
Pretend everything is black when things don't go
your way,
Use the colour grey as an oyster to tap in and tap
out of different states of mind
the next world is only a piece of information
away.

Get lost in yourself, know yourself, learn
yourself because you will never leave you.
You will always need you
You will always see you,
You will always be you.

Tethered

I hope to never come across your successor,
She will find a lived in mind,
Something, somewhere I doubt she could ever
call home,
My senses have been programmed to settings for
functions
that belong to you.

I cannot hear your voice and not want to look,

I cannot look at you and not want to touch,

I cannot touch you and not feel, embrace,
submerge myself in your aura,

Your essence.

I am shackled to an energy that the flesh is a
vehicle to
and freedom would be punishment.

When we are together the world is a bitter
reality,
and I'd rather we stay lost in inception,

Constructing a concrete Eden,

Forever would never be a drag with you.

Carnal Cravings

Lust is so invasive,
Desire is such an intoxicating thought,
Suspending a mind in that state of craving craving craving,
Chasing the moment of climax, the peak of pleasure
Cradle me still when we have melted into each other,
Entangle your limbs with mine, press your skin on my flesh until we are amalgamated by our heat and hearts,
I will rise with your inhale and you will fall with my exhale until I cannot discern your pulse from mine.
Beating beating beating, chime into my rhythm and let the hours go by because time is the only thing that can break this fantasy,
We cannot escape each other's embrace.
We are both one of a kind forging a moment that will bind us long after your tongue would have forgotten the taste.
The pressure on your neck, grip on your thigh, your lips felt between mine, muscle memory

will haunt you, tease you, leave you long enough to have you yearn to be reminded.
You will search for me but their touch will never be true, you will never settle, because we have tasted ecstasy, so go ahead and try, but you will just be chasing the high...

The Path We Choose

The road to freedom is shaded by money trees,
The tongue that talks the tales of freedom has a tinge of hypocrisy,
Hope is hyperbole used like the carrot,
Yet reality hits with the speed of a stick and the force of a brick,
Shift that weight off, find the pace and trace a way out of the concrete confines that reinforce the prison bars in your mind,
Serenghetto strolling,
Seems like the games rigged and these rhymes for now are a lame little gig until I cut-thru and do it big,
Looking for myself as seconds slip away trying to convince myself I'm not losing time,
I'm gaining a new age, new wave,
Manoeuvring in a new way
I got to find the shards of glass that scattered when I hit rock bottom and my life shattered,
Each glass pane is a piece to repaint reshape redefine,
Edit out the pain,

I will create a new tapestry from the ruins of the
last one.
Each new version of me is supposed to be better
than the last one.
My only choice is to improve and enjoy whilst
in use because I don't know which one of me
will be
The last one.

Stockholm Syndrome

Too toxic to be true, too good to be with me,
I'll have to protect you, I performed a falsetto so well you felt it,
But those higher notes are a strain for me to hold, really I'm low, lowly,
Deep and cold, you couldn't handle the bass.
Those vibrations create earthquakes and that's not the way I wanna rock your world.
You've trembled at my tremors and I'm not getting better,
You can only show so much virtue before you seek vendetta and
I love the taste of blood so you can't win for losing.
Far from pure, my tendencies seem to contradict my sentiments,
I'm not present in the moment anymore I'm out of reach,
I'm just a bag of bones,
Someone you've never known with a face that's all too familiar.

I’m unhinged determined to leave someone singed,
Can’t you see my fingertips tinged with venom?
They always sing my praises before crying for mercy and
I always turn pure waters murky.
I learned to sing love songs but no one had to teach me about pain,
and my face glows in the sun but I’ve only ever felt at home in the rain.

A Tour of Insomnia

Feel like a broken record, feel like a broken clock
Build me a time machine, my 3am thoughts have reached dawn and
I haven't even stretched my mouth to yawn,
I'm mourning things that were drawn to a conclusion many moons ago so I should really let go,
It's hard though, the tune is stuck in my head,
It used to be my favourite song now it just keeps me awake in bed,
Louder than the silence that is so deafening -
It's funny how sinister something can be without looking threatening,
The greatest torture is being killed slow
from a strike that was struck from your own blow.
Take me back to the days of bows and arrows,
Point me in the direction of the high sparrow
I will commit myself to nature, God and the ether,
People are too difficult, in fact they make me weaker.

Murder She Wrote

Murder she wrote, I hope she writes me,
Words she would quote, I never took lightly
The spark in her eye, I saw it die quietly,
I could see she could fly, Far she would roam,
Her heart touches mine, She found a home,
But I could not make her stay, I knew she would grow,
Tired of these ways, Away she would go,
All that we are is all that we need, Whatever else we chase feeds narcissistic greed,
I am not tough, I am not clever,
I have no answers, I know no better,
Ignorance is bliss, Information is a burden
A chance that was missed? Lost behind a curtain,
We will speculate, and never be certain,
Much I dismissed to avoid life's turbulence,
The light is a trick but darkness is not permanent.

Your Time Will Come

My lover, it is in your nature to inquire and you found your favourite mystery in me.
Maybe you feel I am something for you to complete,
But you can never be whole if you think I'm the missing piece,
I don't mean to disturb your peace by giving less food for thought about what we could be,
But I've been rocked before, and now I keep a stone face to protect my tranquility,
That means maintaining my keep in the vault that has no key.
I'll give you a bunch of codes to decipher,
I'm cryptic for a reason, I believe 'the one' will connect the dots and wires,
So we'll see what transpires,
I love watching you trying to figure me out,
A few insecurities of mine you helped fish out,
But there's a deeper darker story that I don't want to shed light on,

In the season trees shed their leaves I would end up giving you the cold shoulder to keep myself warmer.

I'm all I've ever had and I've never had to share
So it's not that I don't think you care but
I lose security when you gain a piece of me.
You looking at my insecurities feels like a breach and I don't know how to be fine with you being in reach of everything needed to defeat me.
You feel like the truth in a world of lies,
I'm grateful to have you in this world of mine,
My diamond, daring and divine,
I beam stronger when I feel your shine so I'm letting you know I'm tightly bound,

My armour is woven by pain and pressure,
I will take time to unwind, but one day the way you live in my heart,
You will feel at home in my mind,

Dancing with Danger

I fell in love with the whip,
Infatuated by the sting,
Her tall tales tickled me until I had to smirk,
She accepted my every kink and quirk,
Tippy toed to kiss me and arched her back when I mashed work.
In her ears my deep tone lingered and lurked,
she would place her head on my chest when I spoke just to get richness of the vibrato.
I had the ego of a mogul but she was always better in business,
She knew a transaction when she saw one.
I was lost in emotion chasing a nonexistent notion of amour,
I would negotiate terms but alas, no deal.
If I knew then what I know now would I keel over and reveal what now lays deep down with a seal?
Heal, heal, heal.

Sorry Would Never Be Enough

I forgot more lines about you than I ever wrote down.
Yet still with all the pages covered in your essence there isn't string strong enough I've found that could bound memories I traced of us.

We're stuck in these sad times for the kid,
Both trying to get rid,
But it feels like we're tethered to this force that houses us in all too familiar abyss,
Burdened by turmoil that couldn't give us a miss
Or a break
I pray for your sake
At my best I am a point of relief,
At my worst I am just like them, an addition to the grief.

Self-loathing is hubris in meek's clothing,
I will not be distracted by punishing myself,
I am here to make amends because somewhere along the way I forgot we are not just friends,

We are guardians of each other's soul's until the end.

In Loving Memory of a Burnt Star

You were like an early sunrise from the East in the middle of September,
Warm with all the passions of summer,
Promising more zeal in the coming day with your yellow ambience.
I joined you anticipating hues of orange, my favourite colour,
It was sweet fruit we laboured to enjoy.
Clouds broke up the hours,
For a time it was bleak, but through the murky grey the silver lining kept us tethered.
Light broke through again and we danced under the tangerine sky until it became copper,
We glowed like gold, my fingers only knew silver,
You were kind in the cold,
You did love the ring that slithered, wrapped in each other with no distinguishable end or beginning,
I was suspended in the moment.

Deeper into the night we grew.

Higher into the flight I flew,
Icarus' naïveté riddled me blind to what I saw
When I closed my eyes and saw truth.
Bloodshot, I opened my eyes on impact,
I could only respond tamely because all along I knew.
With all the bright colours removed, that was always you.
It's fades to black and I am home again, alone, all consumed,
Not ashamed or bemused but tickled.
I look at me, we smile, I laugh, we move.

Perspective

I fell in love with her morning face,
and in the evening it was her hips,
In between we talked until there was nothing more to say.
only each other to have and to hold, forever and ever,
So be it until death do us part.
Because life had brought us together,
Our union seemed mystical, tailored by fate
What is written for you, you cannot escape.
When it is sweet, you are the actor on the stage made for you
When it is sour, you are the slave to the system that uses you.
When you are a masochist, you cannot tell the difference.

Wade in the Torture

It was easier to swim before the baggage,
I know I do not have the biggest burden to bare
but of late I merely do not believe I have the
means
to bear it any longer.
Oddly enough I have not fallen to a heavyweight
blow,
But to a storm of thoughts,
Striking me in a melancholy mood,
and I have not been able to get up since,

Sadness is more cruel than death because at least
in death,
There are no shackles.

No memories,

No hope,

No labour,

Give me the spoils of penance and the wages of
sin,
for my toil on Earth has championed misery,
and applauded horror.

Circling the Serenghetto

Stuck in the circus we call life,
Completing the circuit just to keep things aligned,
Keep things right,
When the struggle left us raw and poverty was rife
I toyed with the blade,
Existence was on a knife edge and
I wouldn't be satisfied until I bled,
Because the only feeling we knew was pain.
The only healing we knew was filling you with dread
as we hoped empathy would breed sympathy -
Pack your pity and cut out the headlines that feign piety,
We want change - not movements,
We want to be treated the same not promised - but never given - improvements,
If we don't shake the table we will have to dangle you off a cliff by your ankles
and I cannot think of a more poetic fall from grace.

Deep

The depth of the voice that drags and drains is
carried in waves
micro in size but seismic in the way they stir to
the point hands jitter,
eyes blink at a rapid rate.
There's a twitch that takes over and claws at a
socket,
Gnawing away,
It's biting,
Can you feel parasites chewing away?
Their mouths covered in pink brains 36 degrees
Celsius,
If not over boiled in a skull which I cannot
escape,
Over cooked thoughts from an over cooked
brain
They dribble out in whispers and murmurs
because they lost the bass (base)
Foundations needed to make their way like the
train on a line,
Fares we overpay because a citizen of the earth
has a birthright to reach a place that belongs to
us all,
Flags and anthems separate.
Maniacal mantras grate and grind my gears

Don't cry for war or put fears in chests or put
hearts on sleeves for causes that pluck and feed
on the toil of the naïve to sustain greed.
Put all the things they say you need in a sieve,
Separate the superficial and the beneficial,
The circumstantial and things that are critical in
a state of mind where decisions aren't made in a
fiscal year
See how it all becomes fickle?
If you ever look behind the curtain you may feel
a wetness trickle across a cheek because they
had the cheek to stuff drivel down your throat
and tell you to be thankful for hoofs, intestines
and tails.
Tales,
Tall ones were made to make sure you stayed on
course when they let you set sail,

You are the bottle in the ocean with a message,
Do not look for the shore,
Return to bedrock on sleepless nights
Insomnia stalks - binds dusk and dawn
Fingernails chip on father times cloak,
Plead with him until palms bleed,
There is no way back to (re)write wrongs,
Words fall short like unfinished songs,
Good in intention but without execution all we
see is time gone, opportunity lost,
Never forget what it cost,

Four rights won't make it all disappear but when
you return to where it began
all should be clear.

I Fall For You Quietly

I fall for you Quietly.
When you speak with your heart about the things you love,
When you smile and your eyes beam with infantile innocence,
How your voice doesn't penetrate but instead permeates and all of a sudden I'm wrapped in your tone.
I like how you can snap at me, and I snap back until we stand off eye to eye, then we melt into laughter, because we can't be mad at each other for long enough.
You steady my ship and I'm the wind in your sails,
Bonnie in my whip because you show me where to pass in places I'd struggle to prevail.
Hold me so close you feel my exhale
Skin to skin we sin but this doesn't feel like hell and if it does let the word fall around us.
I'm starting to think with you by my side, things could be just fine.

Be True To Yourself

Don’t be so desperate to feel something you make a bad call,
You’re supposed to be feeling yourself but you’re moving like a free for all the way you responding to everyone’s calls.
If you’re always matching someone else’s energy you’ll never find your own remedy because you’ll pick a poison that may make your heart stall, Or end up on a path where you can’t stand tall because you don’t know how to move unless you crawl,

You weren’t made for the gutter.
Your skin is soon to curdle like butter because you’re tryna bread people just to appease a couple grease balls who got a little cheese. Rats.
Be a skengman or a slewer on your way out of the sewer, I know you’re hungry but your taste is too high for you to settle upon just anything to eat.
Let a pretty girl make your face a seat and try to restore the heat that made you alive.
You were meant to survive,
So thrive.

www.ingramcontent.com/pod-product-compliance
Lightning Source LLC
Chambersburg PA
CBHW051747130826
49812CB00033B/1040
* 9 7 8 9 3 5 7 4 4 5 4 9 8 *